CORN IS MAIZE
The Gift of the Indians

For Alicia, John, Darius, and Noel

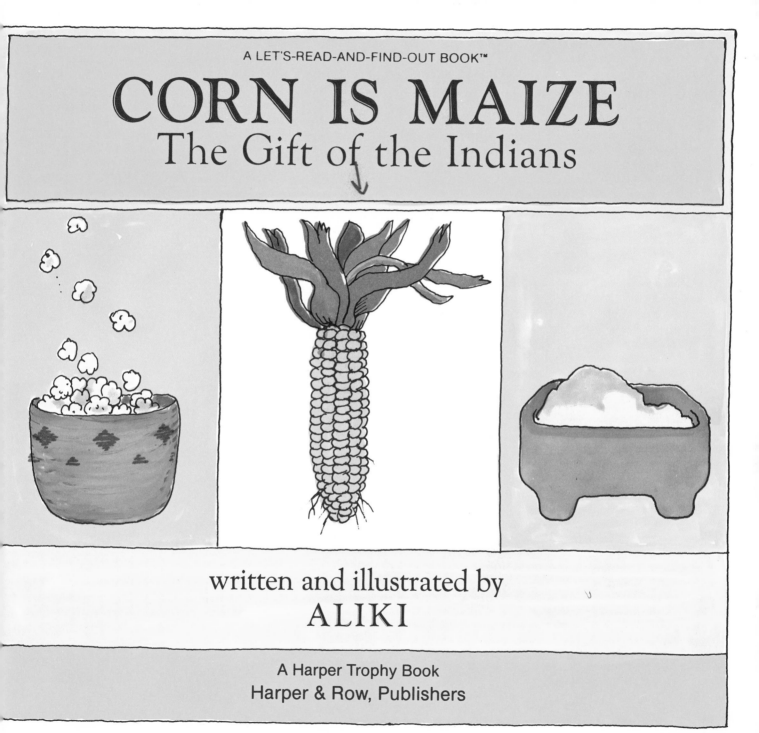

A LET'S-READ-AND-FIND-OUT BOOK™

CORN IS MAIZE
The Gift of the Indians

written and illustrated by
ALIKI

A Harper Trophy Book
Harper & Row, Publishers

LET'S-READ-AND-FIND-OUT BOOKS™

The *Let's-Read-and-Find-Out Book*™ series was originated by Dr. Franklyn M. Branley, Astronomer Emeritus and former Chairman of the American Museum-Hayden Planetarium, and was formerly co-edited by him and Dr. Roma Gans, Professor Emeritus of Childhood Education, Teachers College, Columbia University. Text and illustrations for each of the more than 100 books in the series are checked for accuracy by an expert in the relevant field. Titles available in paperback are listed below. Look for them at your local bookstore or library.

CORN IS MAIZE
The Gift of the Indians

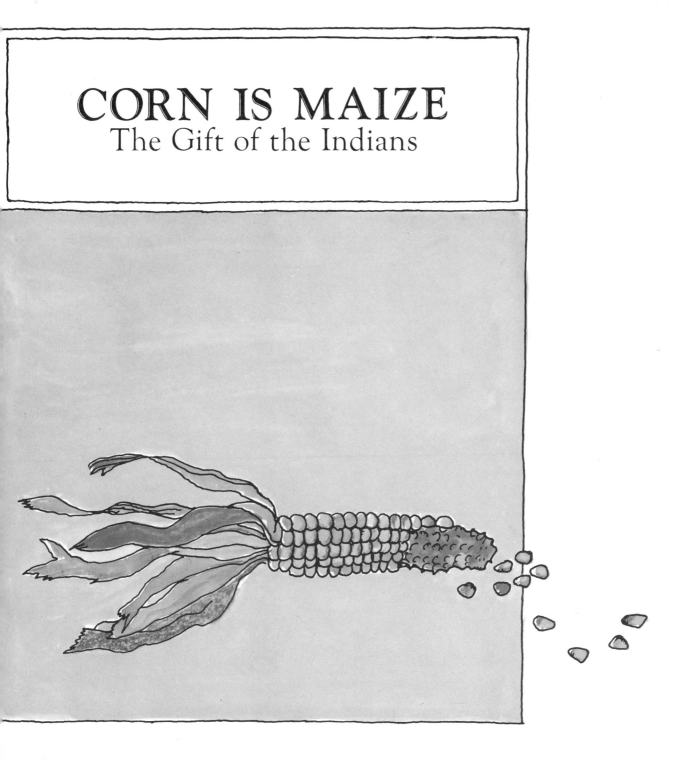

This is a kernel of corn.
It is a corn seed.

Kernels of corn are planted in a small hill of good earth.

The sun shines
down on them.

Spring rains water
the soil.

The hard seeds
soften and sprout.

1

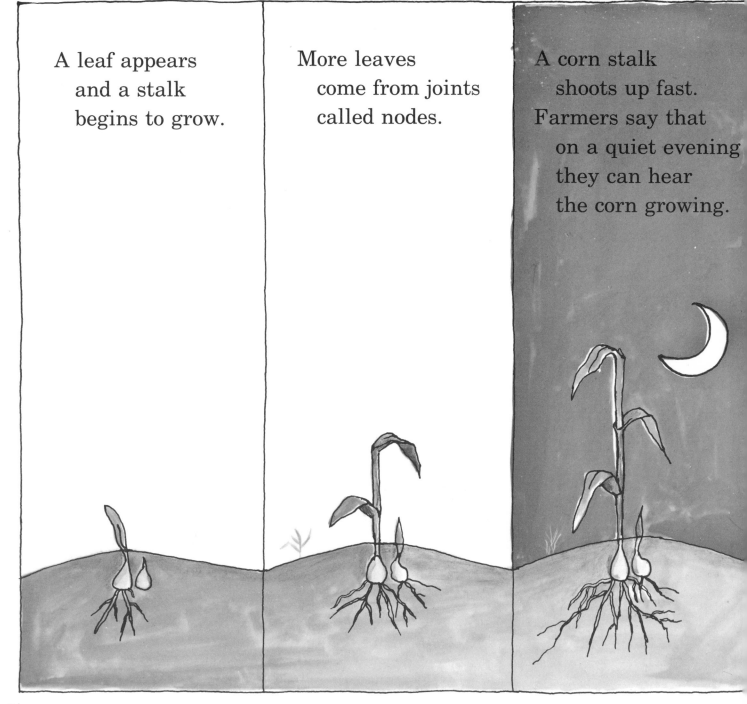

A leaf appears
and a stalk
begins to grow.

More leaves
come from joints
called nodes.

A corn stalk
shoots up fast.
Farmers say that
on a quiet evening
they can hear
the corn growing.

By midsummer, the plant is taller than a farmer.
Husks have begun to sprout from the nodes.
A husk is a bundle of leaves tightly wrapped
  around strands of silk.
  The corn silk is the female part of the plant.
  Tassels grow like a hat at the top of the stalk.
  The tassels are the male flowers.

In the summer breeze, clouds of tiny grains
of pollen blow from the tassels.
The pollen falls on the silk of neighboring corn plants.
Each pollen grain pollinates the strand of silk it sticks to.
After fertilization, a kernel of corn will grow at the
end of each strand.

pollen

corn silk

The pollen travels down the silk.

At the end of each silk is an egg.

corn husk

When the pollen reaches the egg, it pollinates it.

The egg will become a kernel of corn.

egg
corn kernel

The corn husk grows.
Inside the wrapped leaves, hundreds of
    kernels grow into an ear of corn.
The silk turns from a creamy color to
    dark red to brown.

Just before it turns brown, it is time to pick
   the corn and husk it.
The husks and the silk are pulled away.
The sweet, juicy ear of corn is ready
   to cook and eat.

Farmers leave some ears on the stalk.
The brown silk dries.
The kernels harden and are saved.
They are seeds for the next crop.

Many plants can grow wild.
The wind scatters their seeds over
   the earth and they can grow.

Corn kernels cannot fly off the ear
   and scatter.
If an ear fell to the ground, a sprout
   would grow from each kernel.
The new sprouts would grow in a
   tangled heap and die.

Corn cannot grow by itself.
Corn seeds must be planted so there is space around
    each hill for the tall plants to grow.
The plants must be weeded or the baby sprouts
    will be choked.
Corn cannot grow without the help of man.

Then where did corn come from?
How did it start?
For many years there was no answer.
It was a mystery.

Scientists knew corn belongs to the same
   grain family as wheat, rye, oats, barley, and rice.
They are all grass plants.
They all have jointed stems and nodes.
They all grow wild.
But although scientists searched, they had
   never found any wild corn.

wheat

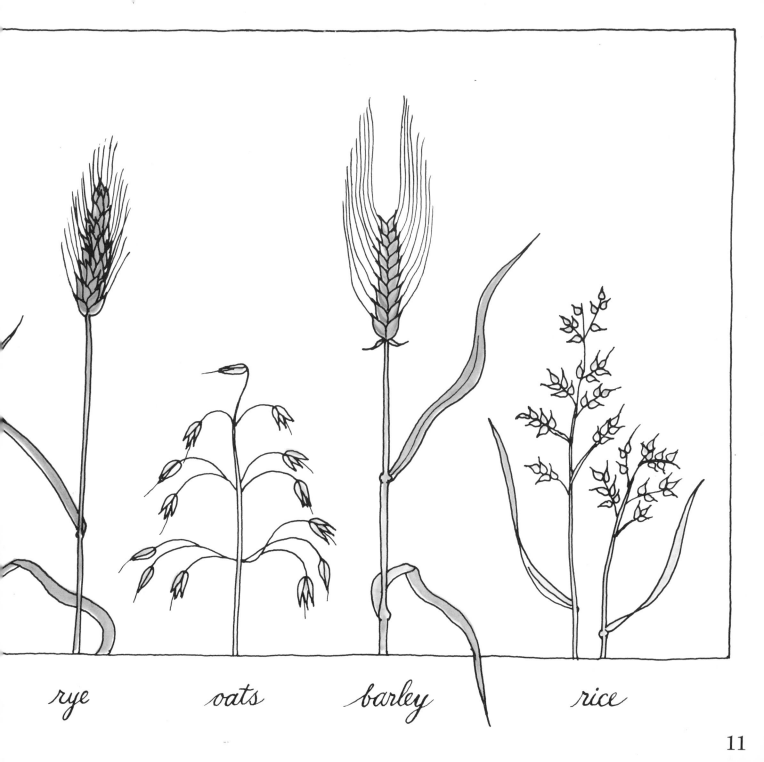

rye   oats   barley   rice

Not long ago they found some.

It was in a cave in Mexico where people once lived.

They found scraps of plants and tiny ears of
    ancient corn, more than 5,000 years old.

It was not like any the scientists had ever seen.

At last they could piece together the story of
  how corn began.

Thousands of years ago, people lived in caves
  in South and Central America.
They planted the seeds of a wild grass,
  perhaps one found in the cave.

Teosinte growing wild.

Scientists think the ancient plant was a tall stalk
with one ear at the top.
The tassel grew out of the ear.
Each tiny orange or brown kernel was wrapped in
its own husk or pod.
The kernels grew so loosely they could fall off the
cob and plant themselves.
The cave dwellers planted and cared for this pod corn.

In time, some scientists think, the pollen of
another grass, called teosinte, or pollen of other
plants, fertilized the corn.
It took hundreds of years for the plants to grow
stronger and the ears larger.

ollen of other plants and teosinte mixed with pod corn to make bigger and bigger ears of corn.

People found the grain was good for them.
It made them stronger than just beans, squash,
   and other plants they knew about.

Tribes in the north began to grow corn, too.
In time, people in all the Americas were growing
   different kinds.
They learned the right time to plant according
   to their climate.

Different tribes planted in different ways.
Some tribes planted five seeds in a hill.
Others planted two.
Some tribes planted bean seeds with the corn
   kernels so the vine could grow up the stalk.
Many tribes learned to bury a fish in each hill.
The fish rotted and made good soil.

By the time Christopher Columbus landed in the New World,
  the people he named "Indians" were expert farmers.
The women tended the crops while the men hunted.
They harvested the corn.
Some of it they ate fresh.
Most of it they dried.
They saved some for seed.
The rest they ground into meal on a
  flat stone called a metate.
They ate the meal dry or made bread with it.
They cooked it into mush.

19

Indians of Mexico used cornmeal to make pancakes
    called tortillas.
They made tamales by wrapping spiced meat
    mixed with meal in husks and boiling them.

Many tribes boiled tiny, tender corn in the husks
    and ate the ears whole.
They ate corn on the cob.
They popped it.

Tribes in the north cooked corn with beans and
    called it misickquatash.
Indians ate the tassels of the corn plant and
    sucked the sweet, fresh stalks.

corn on the cob

popcorn

Misickquatash
known today as
succotash

tortillas

tacos

tamales

corn stalk
"candy"

dry cornmeal

Hidatsa Indians stored corn in the ground.

ashes →
earth →
grass →

They learned to store corn for the
   long winter ahead.
Corn, the Indians' only grain, was their main food.
Their lives depended on it.
Corn was so important to them, the various tribes
   prayed to the Corn Gods they believed had
   sent it to them.

Some Ancient Corn Gods

23

They had festivals at planting time and at harvest.
They chanted and made music, and each tribe
danced its own Corn Dance.

Pueblo Corn Dance
of today

When Christopher Columbus returned to
  Europe he told of the Indians
  and the grain they grew.
He called it maize, which sounded
  like the name the Indians had used.
Even today the correct word for
  corn is maize.

The word "corn" means "grain."
Corn is also the word used for
  the most important grain a
  country grows.
In some countries wheat is called
  corn.
In others, oats are called corn.
The Pilgrims called maize
  "Indian corn," and Americans
  have called it corn ever since.

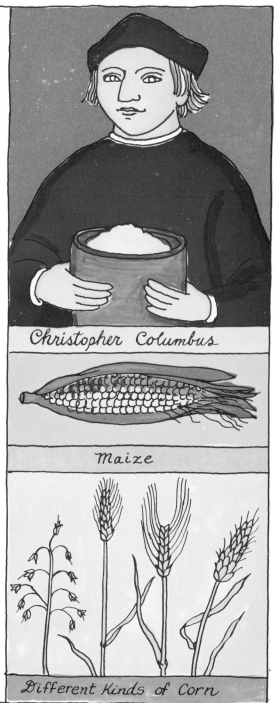

Christopher Columbus

Maize

Different Kinds of Corn

When the Pilgrims landed in America, maize saved
   their lives.
Indians gave them the dried grain to eat and
   showed them how to plant the crop.

On the first Thanksgiving, the Pilgrims and the
   Indians together gave thanks for the corn
   harvest, as the Indians had done long before.

The Pilgrims learned other things from the Indians.
They stuffed mattresses with husks, burned cobs for fuel,

made corncob pipes and corn-shuck dolls, too.

Today people all over the world grow corn.
There are many, many kinds.

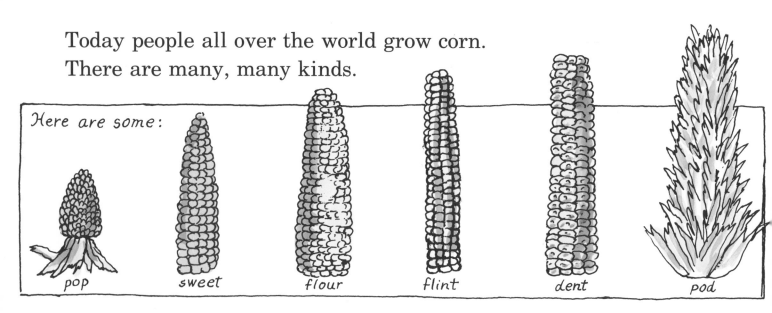

Here are some:

pop   sweet   flour   flint   dent   pod

We eat only sweet corn, and use popcorn for popping.
The rest is used to feed animals and to make:

corn flour   cornmeal   cornstarch   corn oil   corn syrup   cereal

baby powder   glue   soap   alcohol   medicine   .. and many other things.

Now scientists have developed new kinds of corn
   that have more and better protein than any other kind.

People need protein to make them strong and healthy.
Scientists hope someday this new corn will
   help many hungry people in the world.

On large farms today machines help farmers plow
  and sow seeds.
A harvester picks corn and dries it so it can be
  stored without rotting.
Then it is taken to a mill to be ground.

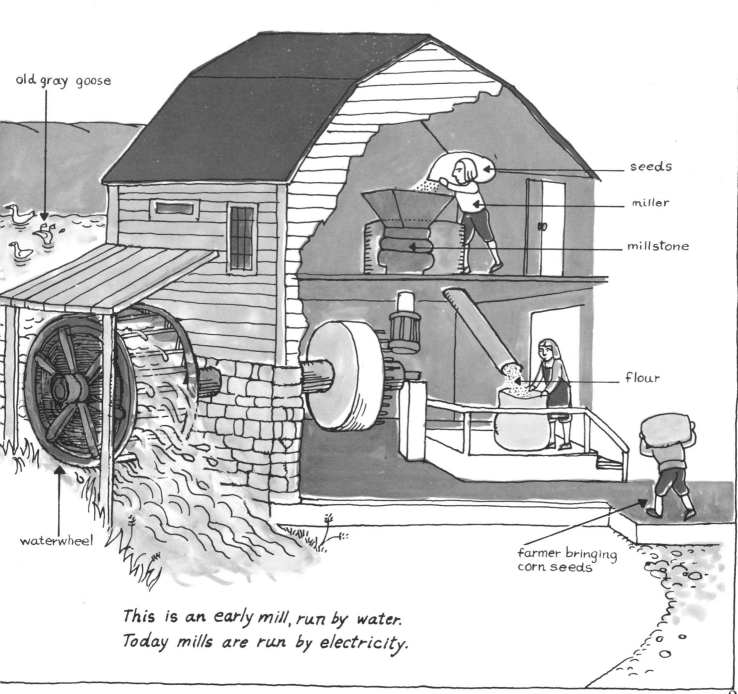

old gray goose

seeds

miller

millstone

flour

farmer bringing
corn seeds

waterwheel

This is an early mill, run by water.
Today mills are run by electricity.

But not all corn is planted and ground by machines.
In parts of America, Indian farmers still grow their corn.
They plant the seeds as their ancestors once did.
They care for the plant, harvest it, and grind
   it on a metate.

And they praise the corn that has fed
their people for thousands of years.

ALIKI'S CORN HUSK DOLL

ABOUT THE AUTHOR-ILLUSTRATOR

Aliki Brandenberg has been fascinated by corn ever since she took her first bite and felt the butter drip down her arm. She also has a great interest in American Indians, their culture and art. In this book, both subjects are brought together.

Mrs. Brandenberg often treats her family to corn fritters, corn bread, and other corn dishes. Then, being a person who throws nothing away, she makes dolls and wreaths with the husks.

1. Bend a wire hanger.

ALIKI'S CORN HUSK WREATH

2. Fold one fresh husk (a) and tie it over hanger (b and c). Repeat and repeat. When wire is full—

3. —use pin to shred. Let it dry.

4. Finished wreath.

DRAGONS
LOVE TACOS

by Adam Rubin
illustrated by Daniel Salmieri

SCHOLASTIC INC.

ISBN 978-0-545-60426-0

Text copyright © 2012 by Adam Rubin.
Illustrations copyright © 2012 by Daniel Salmieri.
All rights reserved. Published by Scholastic Inc.,
557 Broadway, New York, NY 10012,
by arrangement with Dial Books for Young Readers,
a division of Penguin Young Readers Group,
a member of Penguin Group (USA) Inc.
SCHOLASTIC and associated logos are trademarks
and/or registered trademarks of Scholastic Inc.

21   20 21 22/0

Printed in the U.S.A.   40

First Scholastic printing, September 2013

Designed by Jennifer Kelly
Text set in Zemke Hand ITC Std
The artwork was created with watercolor, gouache, and color pencil.

To my loving sister Bruce:
smart, beautiful, and full of laughter.
—AR

For Aaron, a wonderful friend.
Thank you for everything.
—DS

Hey, kid!

Did you know that dragons love tacos?

They love beef tacos and chicken tacos.

They love really big gigantic tacos and tiny
little baby tacos as well.

Why do dragons love tacos?

Maybe it's the smell from the sizzling pan.

Maybe it's the crunch of the crispy tortillas.

Maybe it's a secret.

Either way, if you want to make friends with dragons, tacos are key.

Hey dragon, why do you guys love tacos so much?

But wait!

As much as dragons love tacos, they hate spicy salsa even more.

They hate spicy green salsa and spicy red salsa.

They hate spicy chunky salsa and spicy smooth salsa.

If the salsa is spicy at all, dragons can't stand it.

Why do dragons hate spicy salsa?
Well, just one drop of hot sauce
makes a dragon's ears smoke.

Just one single speck of hot pepper makes a dragon snort sparks.
Spicy salsa gives dragons the tummy troubles,
and when dragons get the tummy troubles—
oh boy . . .

If you want to make tacos for dragons, keep the toppings mild.

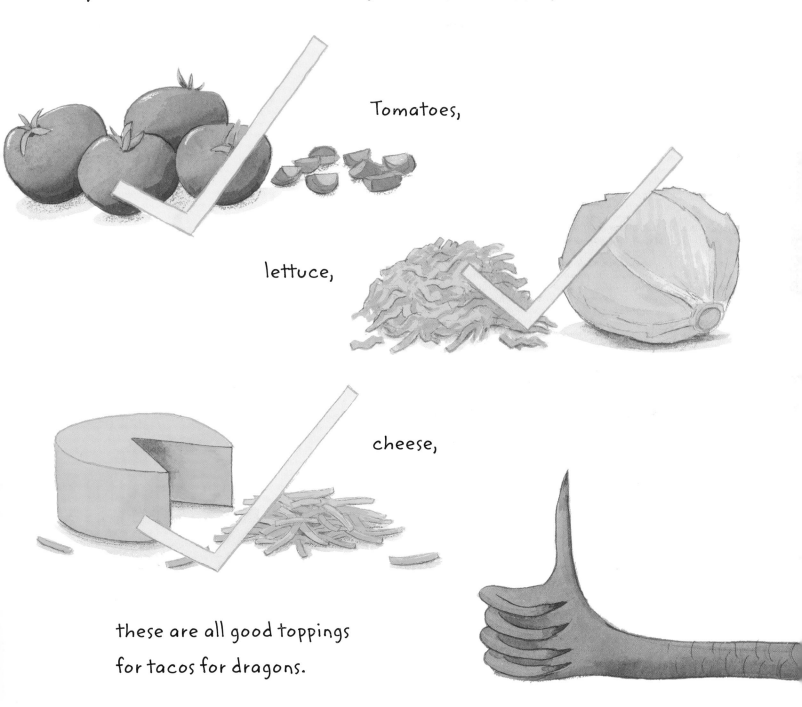

Tomatoes,

lettuce,

cheese,

these are all good toppings
for tacos for dragons.

Hey dragon, how do you feel about spicy taco toppings?

Dragons love parties. They like costume parties

and pool parties.

They like big gigantic parties with accordions

and tiny little parties with charades.

Why do dragons love parties? Maybe it's the conversation. Maybe it's the dancing. Maybe it's the comforting sound of a good friend's laughter.

The only thing dragons love more than parties or tacos, is taco parties (taco parties are parties with lots of tacos).

If you want to have some dragons over for a taco party, you'll need buckets of tacos. Pantloads of tacos. The best way to judge is to get a boat and fill the boat with tacos. That's about how many tacos dragons need for a taco party. After all, dragons love tacos.

Hey dragon, are you excited for the big taco party?

Just remember: Dragons hate spicy salsa.
Before you host your taco party with dragons,
get rid of all the spicy salsa. In fact, bury the spicy
salsa in the backyard so the dragons can't find it.

These dragons love your taco party! They love the music.
They love the decorations. They especially love the tacos.

Congratulations!

It's a good thing you got rid of all that spicy . . .

Wait a second—
what are those little green things in the salsa?
You didn't read the fine print?!

Dragons, listen to me: Do not eat those tacos.

Those little green specs in the salsa? Those are jalapeño peppers—they are super-spicy! I know you love tacos, dragons, but you are not gonna love those tacos.

DO NOT LET THOSE DRAGONS EAT THOSE TACOS!!!

Crunch,   crunch,   crunch . . .

Why would dragons help you rebuild your house?

Maybe they're good Samaritans.

Maybe they feel bad for wrecking it.

Maybe they're just in it for the taco breaks.

After all, dragons love tacos.